L S Lowry

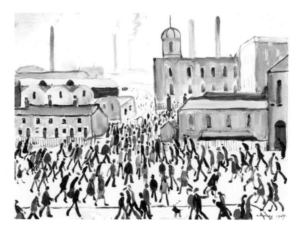

DIARY **2024**

The Lowry is one of the UK's leading cultural institutions; a registered charity with a commitment to enriching people's lives through access to the arts; and a cornerstone of the regeneration of Salford Quays.

In its galleries, The Lowry houses the world's largest permanent collection of paintings and drawings by L.S. Lowry and also cares for and maintains the artist's archive of exhibition catalogues, press cuttings, letters, photographs and items including Lowry's paint brushes and palette knives. Alongside this, it regularly commissions new work from contemporary artists for its special exhibition programme. On its stages, The Lowry presents work from local, national and international companies; including that of its Partners, Birmingham Royal Ballet, the National Theatre, Opera North and Rambert. The Lowry's learning and engagement programme is primarily aimed at communities across the city of Salford, with a focus on young people; including those acting as carers to other family members, those that are – or have been – in the care system or those with autism and additional needs.

For more information visit www.thelowry.com

First published in 2023

Created and Published by
FLAME TREE PUBLISHING
6 Melbray Mews,
London SW6 3NS, UK
Tel: +44 (0) 20 7751 9650
info@flametreepublishing.com
www.flametreepublishing.com

ISBN: 978-1-80417-492-0

All works by L.S. Lowry (1887–1976)
© The Lowry Collection, Salford

Front cover: *Going to Work*, 1959 (detail)
Back cover: *A Fight*, c. 1935 (detail)

Every attempt has been made to ensure the accuracy of the date information at the time of going
to press, and the publishers cannot accept responsibility for any errors. Some public holidays are subject
to change by Royal or State proclamation. At the time of publication, accurate information was unavailable
for all religious celebrations in 2024. All Jewish and Islamic holidays begin at sunset on the previous
day and end at sunset on the date shown. Moon phases are based on GMT.

Every effort has been made to contact all copyright holders. The publishers
would be pleased to hear if any oversights or omissions have occurred.

Created and published in the UK. Printed in China.

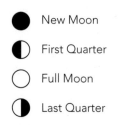

New Moon

First Quarter

Full Moon

Last Quarter

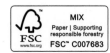

2023

JANUARY
S	M	T	W	T	F	S
1	2	3	4	5	6	7
8	9	10	11	12	13	14
15	16	17	18	19	20	21
22	23	24	25	26	27	28
29	30	31				

FEBRUARY
S	M	T	W	T	F	S
			1	2	3	4
5	6	7	8	9	10	11
12	13	14	15	16	17	18
19	20	21	22	23	24	25
26	27	28				

MARCH
S	M	T	W	T	F	S
			1	2	3	4
5	6	7	8	9	10	11
12	13	14	15	16	17	18
19	20	21	22	23	24	25
26	27	28	29	30	31	

APRIL
S	M	T	W	T	F	S
						1
2	3	4	5	6	7	8
9	10	11	12	13	14	15
16	17	18	19	20	21	22
23	24	25	26	27	28	29
30						

MAY
S	M	T	W	T	F	S
	1	2	3	4	5	6
7	8	9	10	11	12	13
14	15	16	17	18	19	20
21	22	23	24	25	26	27
28	29	30	31			

JUNE
S	M	T	W	T	F	S
				1	2	3
4	5	6	7	8	9	10
11	12	13	14	15	16	17
18	19	20	21	22	23	24
25	26	27	28	29	30	

JULY
S	M	T	W	T	F	S
						1
2	3	4	5	6	7	8
9	10	11	12	13	14	15
16	17	18	19	20	21	22
23	24	25	26	27	28	29
30	31					

AUGUST
S	M	T	W	T	F	S
		1	2	3	4	5
6	7	8	9	10	11	12
13	14	15	16	17	18	19
20	21	22	23	24	25	26
27	28	29	30	31		

SEPTEMBER
S	M	T	W	T	F	S
					1	2
3	4	5	6	7	8	9
10	11	12	13	14	15	16
17	18	19	20	21	22	23
24	25	26	27	28	29	30

OCTOBER
S	M	T	W	T	F	S
1	2	3	4	5	6	7
8	9	10	11	12	13	14
15	16	17	18	19	20	21
22	23	24	25	26	27	28
29	30	31				

NOVEMBER
S	M	T	W	T	F	S
			1	2	3	4
5	6	7	8	9	10	11
12	13	14	15	16	17	18
19	20	21	22	23	24	25
26	27	28	29	30		

DECEMBER
S	M	T	W	T	F	S
					1	2
3	4	5	6	7	8	9
10	11	12	13	14	15	16
17	18	19	20	21	22	23
24	25	26	27	28	29	30
31						

2024

JANUARY
S	M	T	W	T	F	S
	1	2	3	4	5	6
7	8	9	10	11	12	13
14	15	16	17	18	19	20
21	22	23	24	25	26	27
28	29	30	31			

FEBRUARY
S	M	T	W	T	F	S
				1	2	3
4	5	6	7	8	9	10
11	12	13	14	15	16	17
18	19	20	21	22	23	24
25	26	27	28	29		

MARCH
S	M	T	W	T	F	S
					1	2
3	4	5	6	7	8	9
10	11	12	13	14	15	16
17	18	19	20	21	22	23
24	25	26	27	28	29	30
31						

APRIL
S	M	T	W	T	F	S
	1	2	3	4	5	6
7	8	9	10	11	12	13
14	15	16	17	18	19	20
21	22	23	24	25	26	27
28	29	30				

MAY
S	M	T	W	T	F	S
			1	2	3	4
5	6	7	8	9	10	11
12	13	14	15	16	17	18
19	20	21	22	23	24	25
26	27	28	29	30	31	

JUNE
S	M	T	W	T	F	S
						1
2	3	4	5	6	7	8
9	10	11	12	13	14	15
16	17	18	19	20	21	22
23	24	25	26	27	28	29
30						

JULY
S	M	T	W	T	F	S
	1	2	3	4	5	6
7	8	9	10	11	12	13
14	15	16	17	18	19	20
21	22	23	24	25	26	27
28	29	30	31			

AUGUST
S	M	T	W	T	F	S
				1	2	3
4	5	6	7	8	9	10
11	12	13	14	15	16	17
18	19	20	21	22	23	24
25	26	27	28	29	30	31

SEPTEMBER
S	M	T	W	T	F	S
1	2	3	4	5	6	7
8	9	10	11	12	13	14
15	16	17	18	19	20	21
22	23	24	25	26	27	28
29	30					

OCTOBER
S	M	T	W	T	F	S
		1	2	3	4	5
6	7	8	9	10	11	12
13	14	15	16	17	18	19
20	21	22	23	24	25	26
27	28	29	30	31		

NOVEMBER
S	M	T	W	T	F	S
					1	2
3	4	5	6	7	8	9
10	11	12	13	14	15	16
17	18	19	20	21	22	23
24	25	26	27	28	29	30

DECEMBER
S	M	T	W	T	F	S
1	2	3	4	5	6	7
8	9	10	11	12	13	14
15	16	17	18	19	20	21
22	23	24	25	26	27	28
29	30	31				

2025

JANUARY
S	M	T	W	T	F	S
			1	2	3	4
5	6	7	8	9	10	11
12	13	14	15	16	17	18
19	20	21	22	23	24	25
26	27	28	29	30	31	

FEBRUARY
S	M	T	W	T	F	S
						1
2	3	4	5	6	7	8
9	10	11	12	13	14	15
16	17	18	19	20	21	22
23	24	25	26	27	28	

MARCH
S	M	T	W	T	F	S
						1
2	3	4	5	6	7	8
9	10	11	12	13	14	15
16	17	18	19	20	21	22
23	24	25	26	27	28	29
30	31					

APRIL
S	M	T	W	T	F	S
		1	2	3	4	5
6	7	8	9	10	11	12
13	14	15	16	17	18	19
20	21	22	23	24	25	26
27	28	29	30			

MAY
S	M	T	W	T	F	S
				1	2	3
4	5	6	7	8	9	10
11	12	13	14	15	16	17
18	19	20	21	22	23	24
25	26	27	28	29	30	31

JUNE
S	M	T	W	T	F	S
1	2	3	4	5	6	7
8	9	10	11	12	13	14
15	16	17	18	19	20	21
22	23	24	25	26	27	28
29	30					

JULY
S	M	T	W	T	F	S
		1	2	3	4	5
6	7	8	9	10	11	12
13	14	15	16	17	18	19
20	21	22	23	24	25	26
27	28	29	30	31		

AUGUST
S	M	T	W	T	F	S
					1	2
3	4	5	6	7	8	9
10	11	12	13	14	15	16
17	18	19	20	21	22	23
24	25	26	27	28	29	30
31						

SEPTEMBER
S	M	T	W	T	F	S
	1	2	3	4	5	6
7	8	9	10	11	12	13
14	15	16	17	18	19	20
21	22	23	24	25	26	27
28	29	30				

OCTOBER
S	M	T	W	T	F	S
			1	2	3	4
5	6	7	8	9	10	11
12	13	14	15	16	17	18
19	20	21	22	23	24	25
26	27	28	29	30	31	

NOVEMBER
S	M	T	W	T	F	S
						1
2	3	4	5	6	7	8
9	10	11	12	13	14	15
16	17	18	19	20	21	22
23	24	25	26	27	28	29
30						

DECEMBER
S	M	T	W	T	F	S
	1	2	3	4	5	6
7	8	9	10	11	12	13
14	15	16	17	18	19	20
21	22	23	24	25	26	27
28	29	30	31			

The Lake, 1951 (detail)
Oil on board

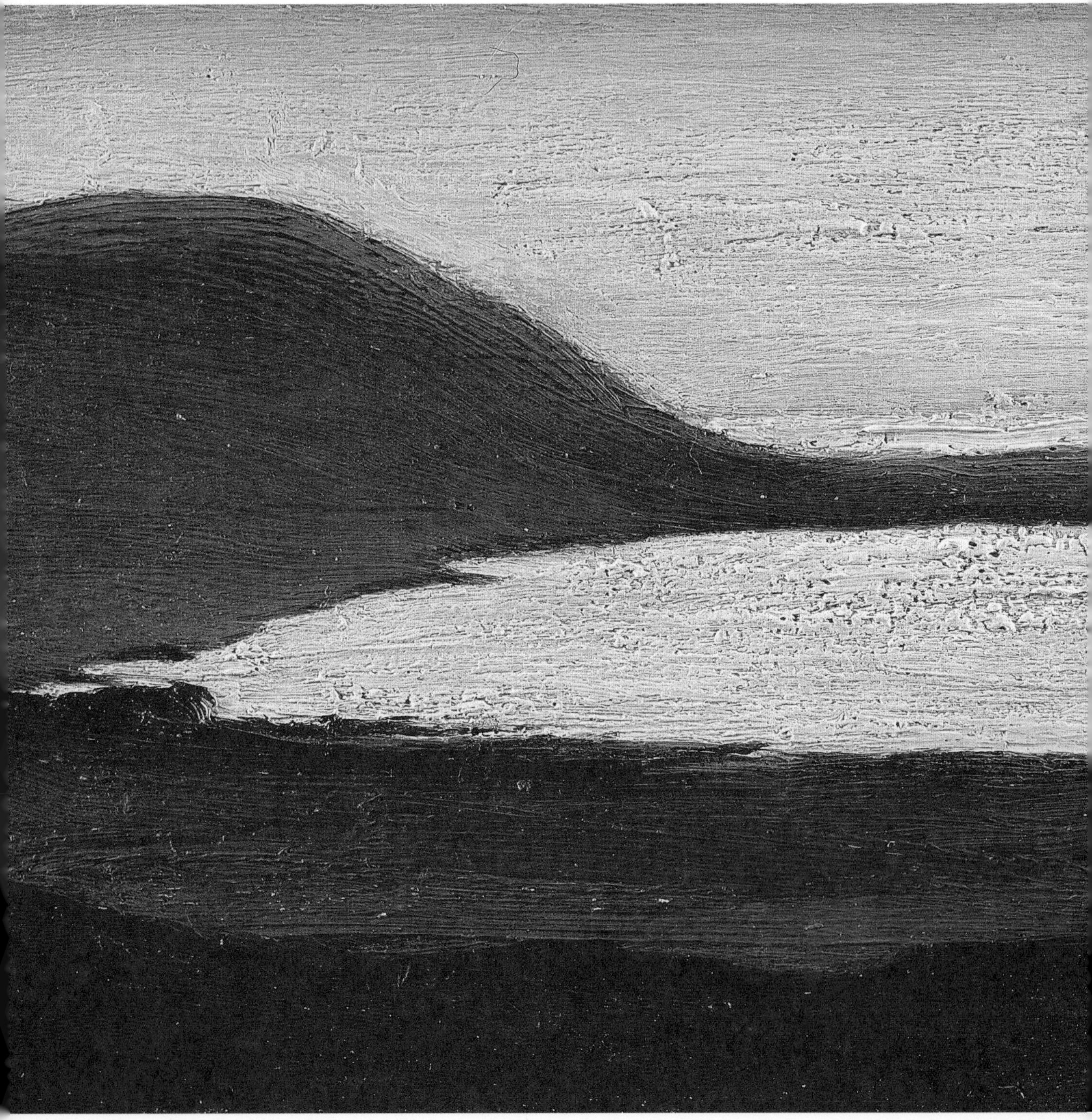

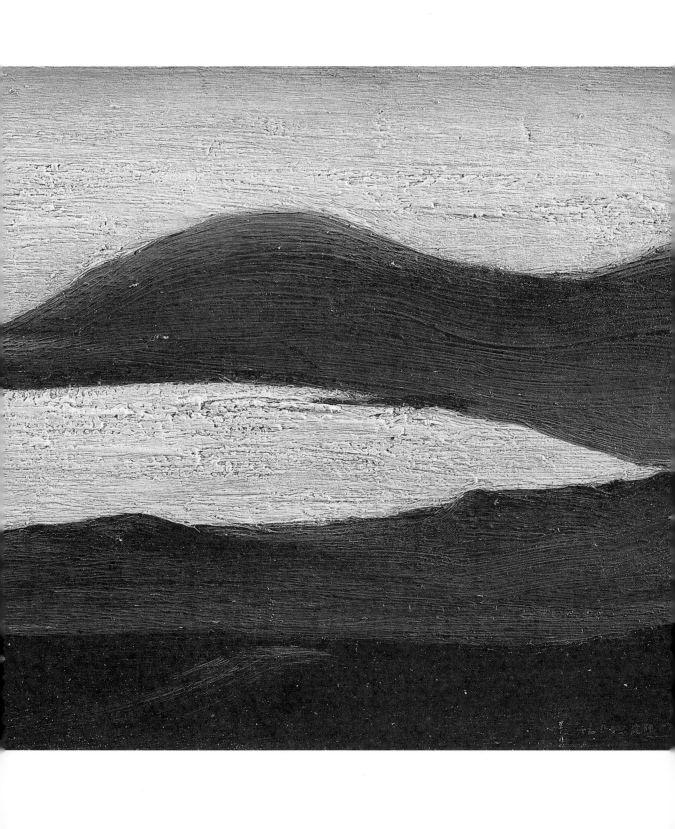

Personal Information

Name

Address

Telephone

Mobile

Work Telephone

Email

Bank Telephone

Credit Card Telephone

National Insurance No.

Passport No.

Driving Licence No.

AA or RAC Membership No.

In Case of Emergency

Contact

Telephone

Doctor

Known Allergies

Notes

January

1 Monday

New Year's Day

2 Tuesday

Public Holiday (Scot, NZ)

3 Wednesday

4 Thursday ◐

5 Friday

6 Saturday

ANL

+ WN PB 10-7

Epiphany
Three Kings' Day

7 Sunday

ANL

January

---

8 Monday

Back @ School

---

9 Tuesday

---

10 Wednesday

---

11 Thursday

---

12 Friday

---

13 Saturday

---

14 Sunday

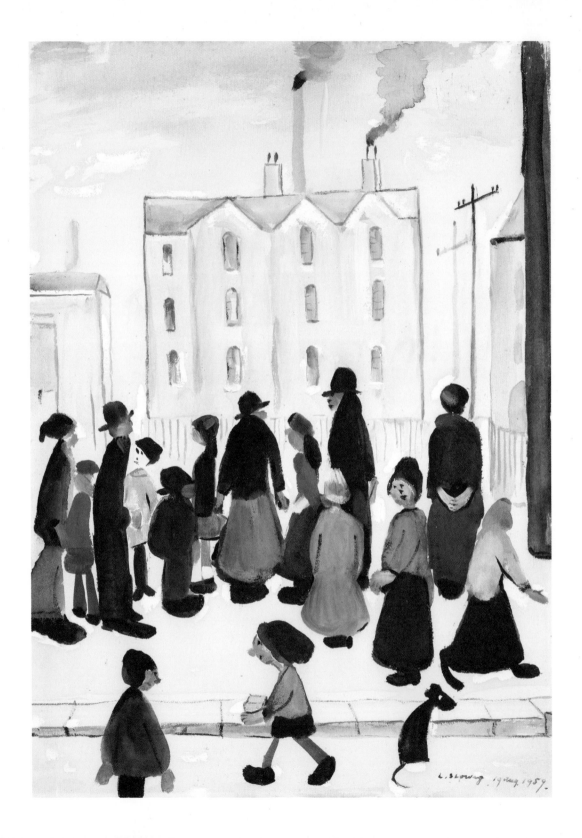

January

15 Monday

Martin Luther King Jr Day (USA)

16 Tuesday

17 Wednesday

Birthday of Guru Gobind Singh

18 Thursday

19 Friday

20 Saturday

21 Sunday

Group of People, 1959
Watercolour on paper

January

22 Monday

23 Tuesday

24 Wednesday

25 Thursday ○

Burns Night (Scot)

26 Friday

Australia Day

27 Saturday

28 Sunday

House on the Moor, 1950
Oil on canvas

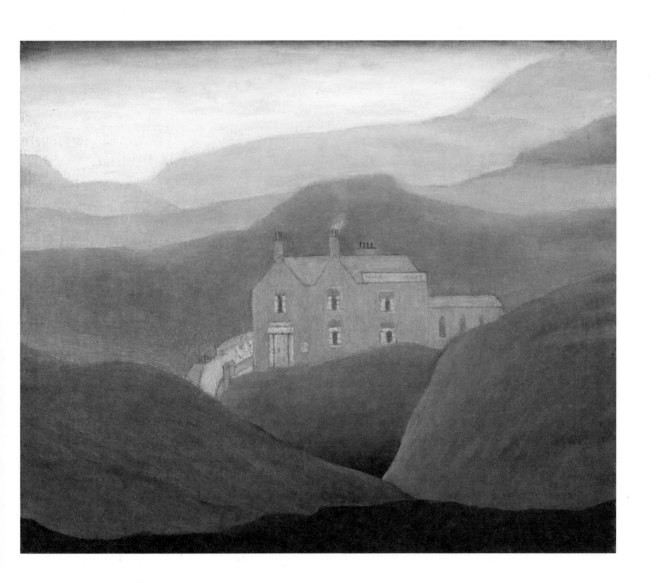

January/February

29 Monday

30 Tuesday

31 Wednesday

1 Thursday

2 Friday ◑

Groundhog Day (USA, Canada)

3 Saturday

4 Sunday

February

---

5 Monday

---

6 Tuesday

Waitangi Day (NZ)

7 Wednesday

---

8 Thursday

● 9 Friday

---

10 Saturday

Chinese New Year
Year of the Dragon

11 Sunday

National Foundation Day (Japan)

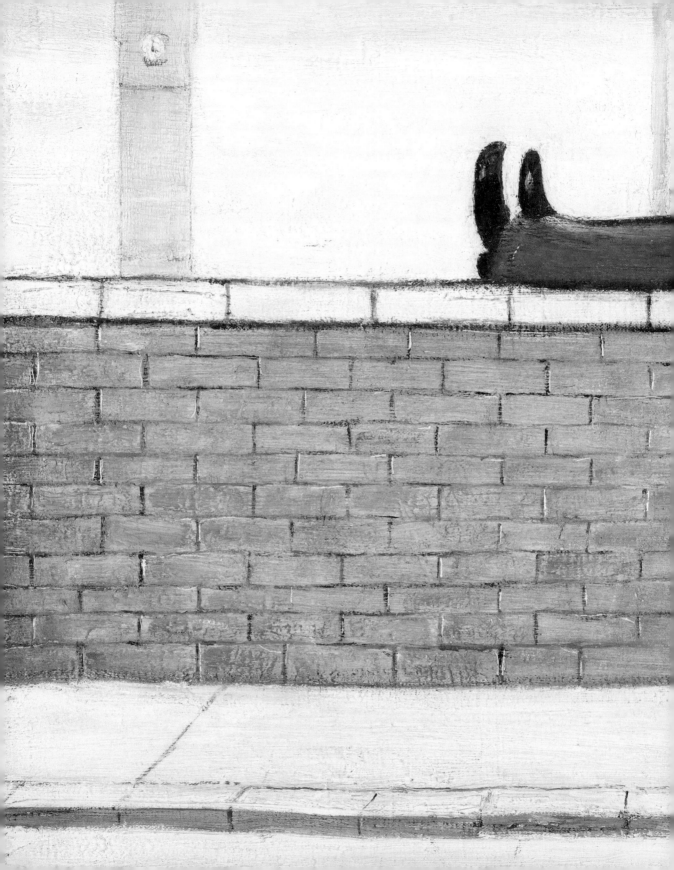

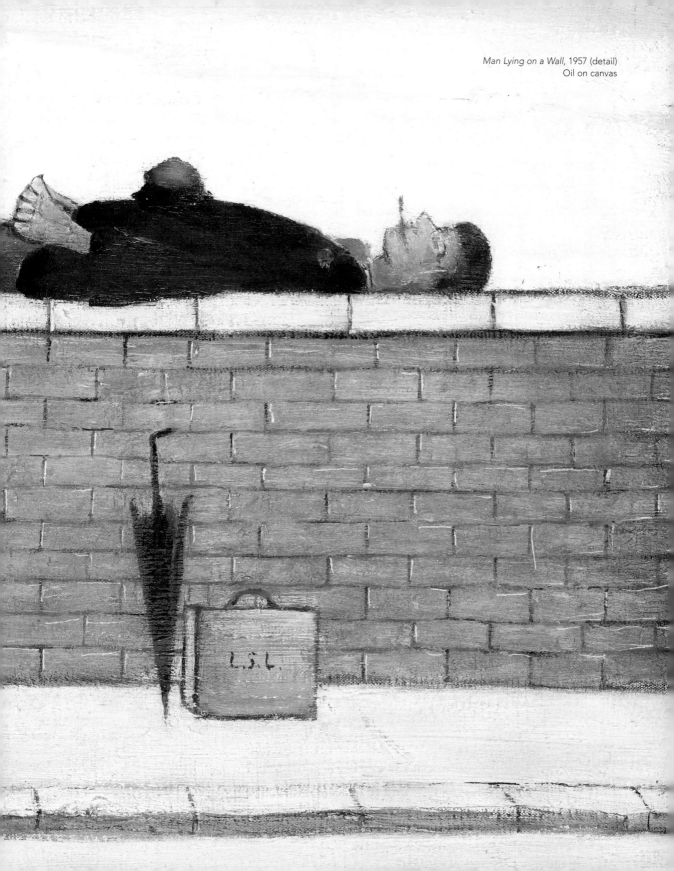

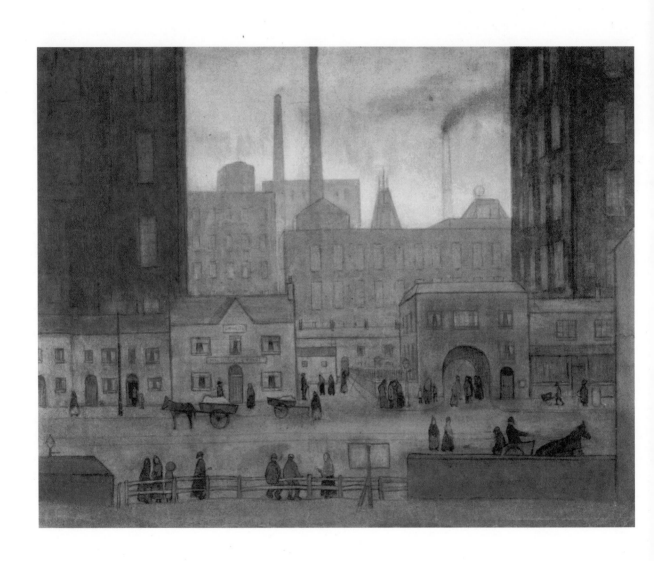

WEEK **7**

February

---

12 Monday

National Foundation Day (Japan) (observed)

---

13 Tuesday

Shrove Tuesday
Pancake Day

---

14 Wednesday

St Valentine's Day
Ash Wednesday
Vasant Panchami

---

15 Thursday

◑ **16 Friday**

---

17 Saturday

---

18 Sunday

First Sunday of Lent

Coming from the Mill, c. 1917–18
Pastel on paper

February

19 Monday

Presidents' Day (USA)
Family Day (Canada)

20 Tuesday

21 Wednesday

22 Thursday

23 Friday

The Emperor's Birthday (Japan)

24 Saturday

○

25 Sunday

The Steps, Peel Park, Salford, 1930
Pencil on paper

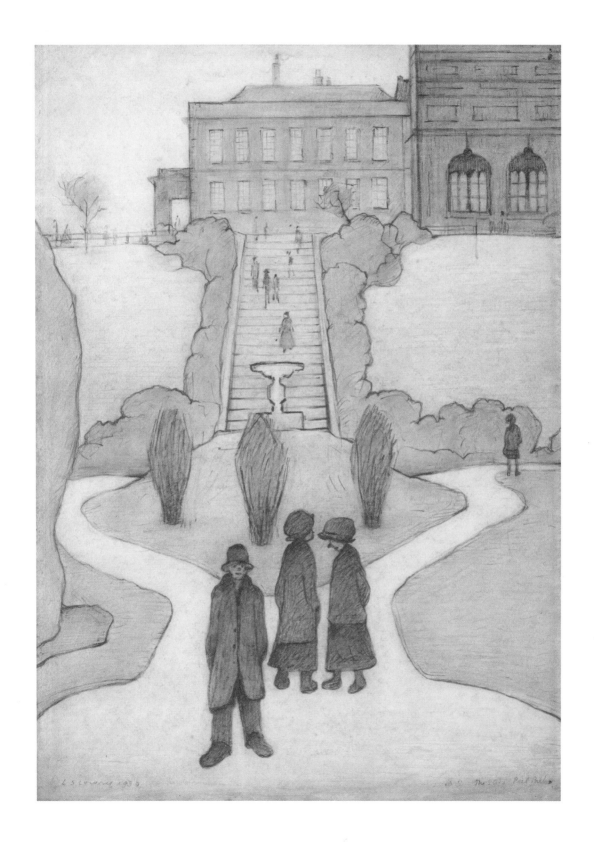

February/March

26 Monday

27 Tuesday

28 Wednesday

29 Thursday

1 Friday

St David's Day (Wales)

2 Saturday

3 Sunday

March

4 Monday

5 Tuesday

6 Wednesday

7 Thursday

8 Friday

Maha Shivaratri
International Women's Day

9 Saturday

● 10 Sunday

Mother's Day (UK, Éire)

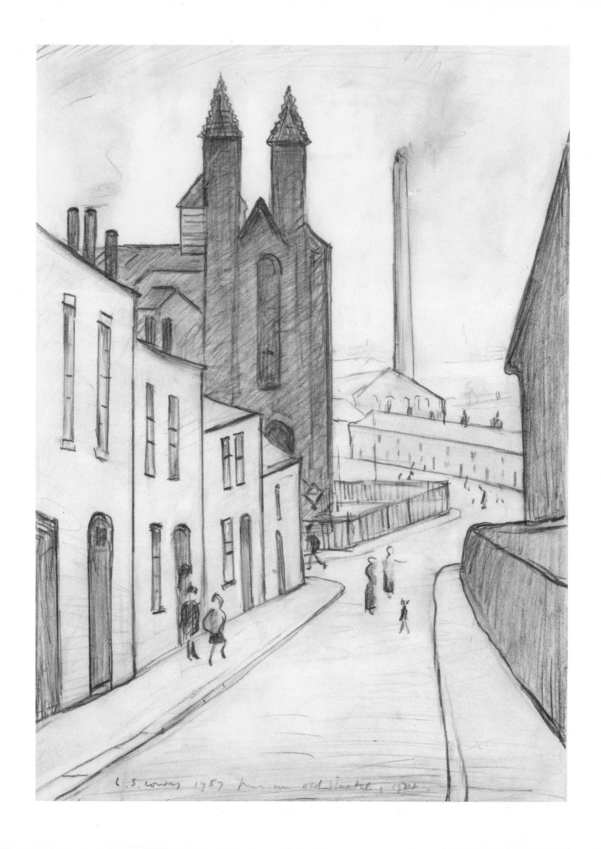

L. S. Lowry 1957 from an old sketch, 1924.

March

11 Monday

Ramadan begins
Commonwealth Day

12 Tuesday

13 Wednesday

14 Thursday

15 Friday

16 Saturday

◑ 17 Sunday

St Patrick's Day

Richmond Hill, 1957
Pencil on paper

March

---

18 Monday

St Patrick's Day (N. Ireland) (observed)

19 Tuesday

---

20 Wednesday

Spring Equinox

21 Thursday

Hindi New Year
Human Rights Day (SA)

22 Friday

---

23 Saturday

---

24 Sunday

Purim
Palm Sunday

Chapel, St Stephen's Church, Salford, 1956
Pencil on paper

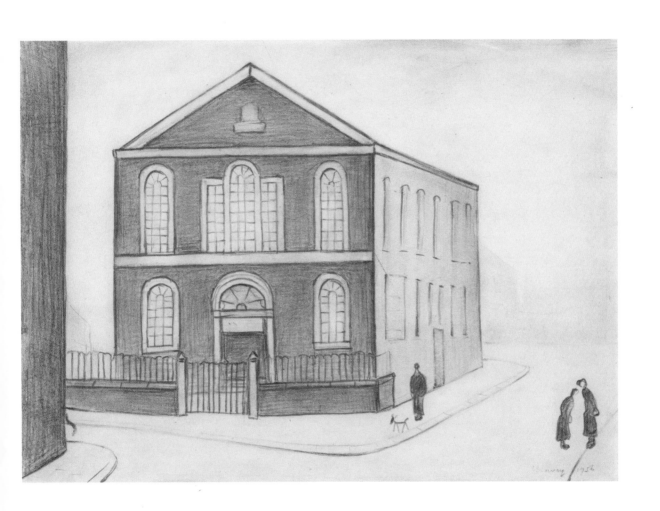

March

25 Monday

○

Holi
Hola Mohalla begins

26 Tuesday

27 Wednesday

Hola Mohalla ends

28 Thursday

Maundy Thursday

29 Friday

Good Friday

30 Saturday

31 Sunday

Easter Sunday
British Summer Time begins

WEEK **14**

April

1 Monday

Easter Monday
Family Day (SA)

◐ 2 Tuesday

3 Wednesday

4 Thursday

5 Friday

6 Saturday

7 Sunday

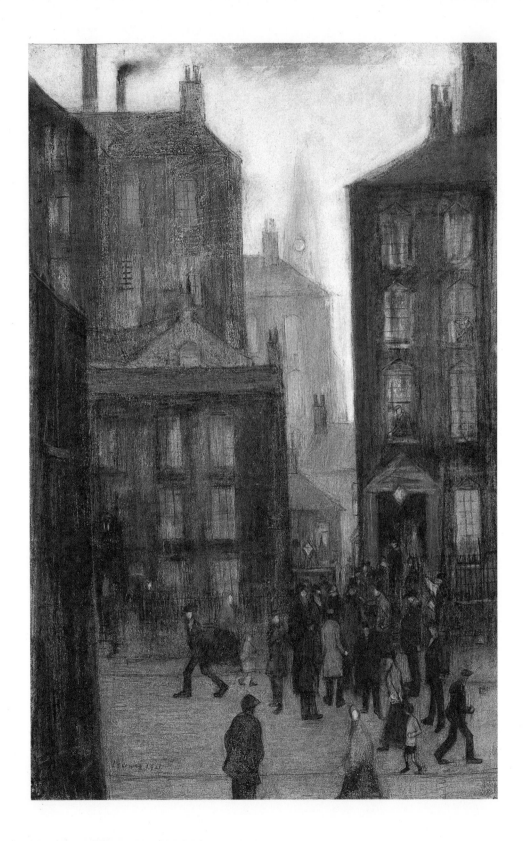

April

---

8 Monday

●

---

9 Tuesday

Ramadan ends
Ramayana Week begins

---

10 Wednesday

Eid al-Fitr

---

11 Thursday

---

12 Friday

---

13 Saturday

Vaisakhi

14 Sunday

The Lodging House, 1921
Pastel on paper

April

15 Monday ◐

16 Tuesday

17 Wednesday

Rama Navami

18 Thursday

19 Friday

20 Saturday

21 Sunday

Bandstand, Peel Park, Salford, 1925
Pencil on paper

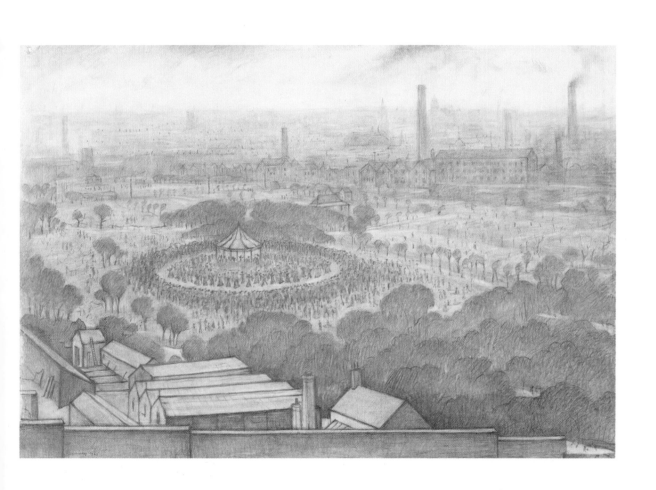

April

22 Monday

23 Tuesday ○

Hanuman Jayanti
St George's Day (England)
First Day of Passover (Pesach)

24 Wednesday

25 Thursday

Anzac Day (AU, NZ)

26 Friday

27 Saturday

Freedom Day (SA)

28 Sunday

April/May

29 Monday

Shōwa Day (Japan)

30 Tuesday

Last Day of Passover (Pesach)

1 Wednesday

Workers' Day (SA)

2 Thursday

3 Friday

Constitution Memorial Day (Japan)

4 Saturday

Greenery Day (Japan)

5 Sunday

Children's Day (Japan)

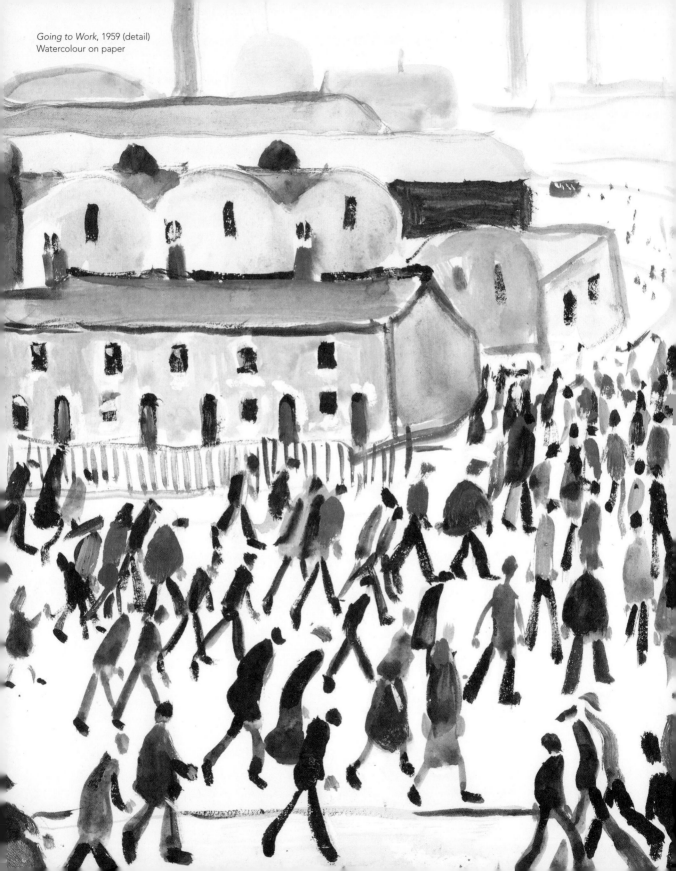

Going to Work, 1959 (detail)
Watercolour on paper

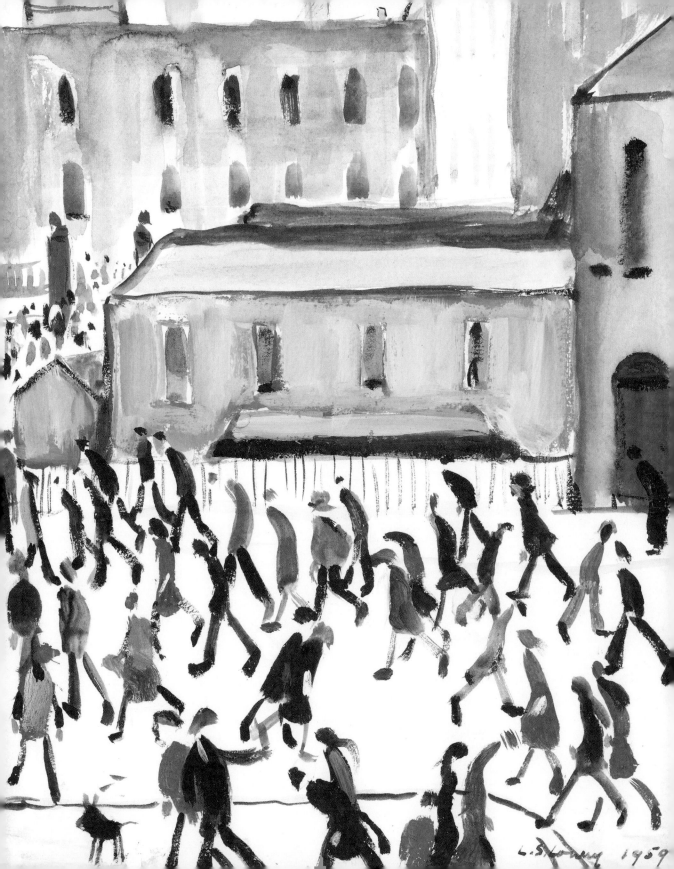

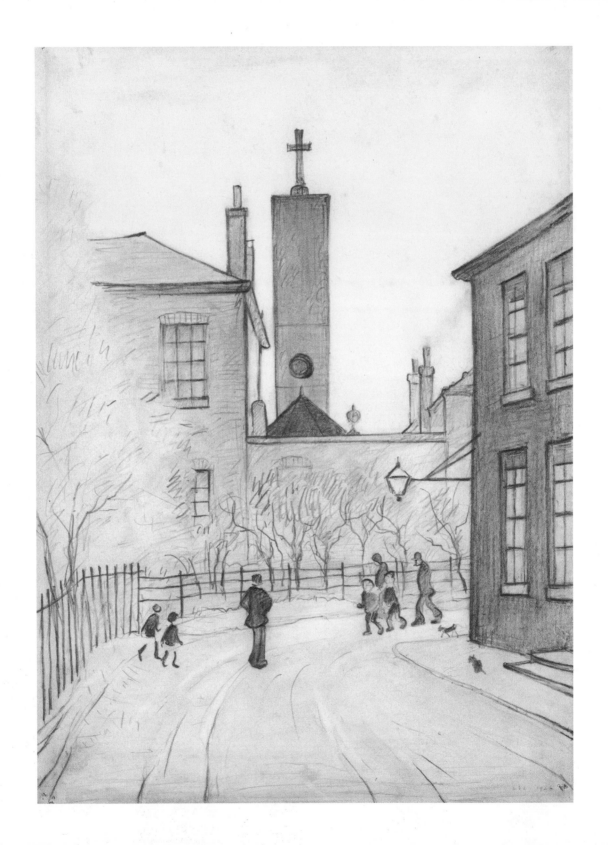

May

6 Monday

Coronation Day (UK)
May Bank Holiday (UK, Éire)
Children's Day (Japan) (observed)

7 Tuesday

● 8 Wednesday

9 Thursday

Ascension Day

10 Friday

11 Saturday

12 Sunday

Mother's Day (USA, Canada, AU, NZ, SA, Japan)

The Tower, 1926
Pencil on paper

May

13 Monday

14 Tuesday

15 Wednesday ◑

16 Thursday

17 Friday

18 Saturday

19 Sunday

Pentecost

Waiting for the Newspapers, 1930
Pencil on paper

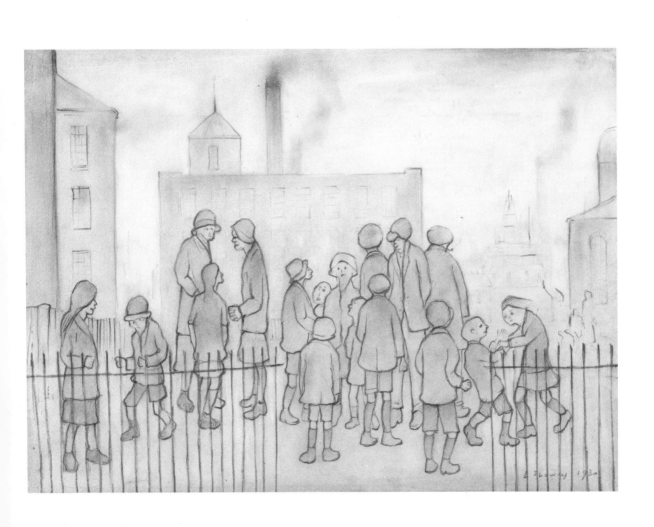

May

20 Monday

Whit Monday
Victoria Day (Canada)

21 Tuesday

22 Wednesday

23 Thursday   ○

Vesak Day

24 Friday

25 Saturday

26 Sunday

Trinity Sunday

May/June

27 Monday

Memorial Day (USA)
Spring Bank Holiday (UK)

28 Tuesday

29 Wednesday

◑ 30 Thursday

Corpus Christi

31 Friday

1 Saturday

2 Sunday

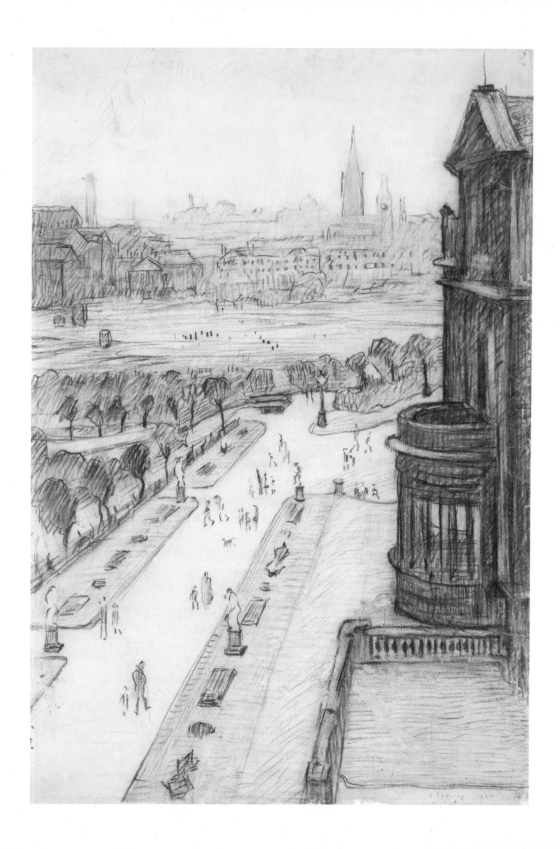

June

---

3 Monday

June Bank Holiday (Éire)

4 Tuesday

---

5 Wednesday

● 6 Thursday

---

7 Friday

---

8 Saturday

The King's Official Birthday (UK)

9 Sunday

A View from the Window of the Royal Technical College, Salford, Looking Towards Manchester, 1921
Black chalk and pencil on paper

June

---

10 Monday

Dragon Boat Festival

11 Tuesday

---

12 Wednesday

Shavuot begins

13 Thursday

Shavuot ends

14 Friday　　◑

---

15 Saturday

---

16 Sunday

Youth Day (SA)
Martyrdom of Guru Arjan Dev
Father's Day (UK, Éire, USA, Canada, SA, Japan)

A Landmark, 1936
Oil on canvas

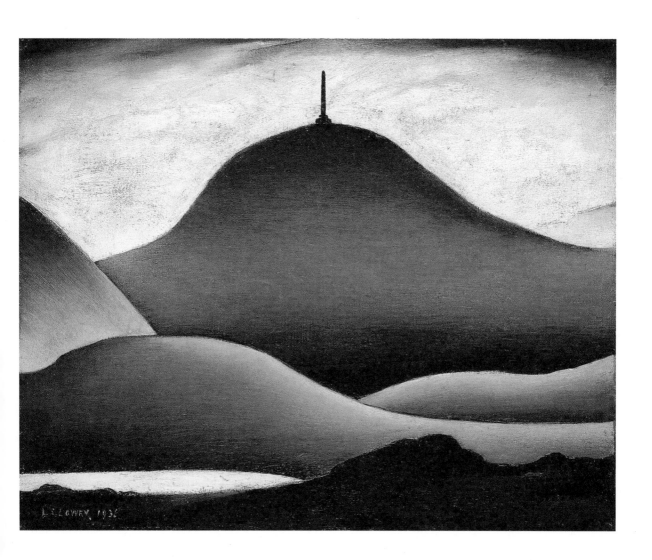

June

17 Monday

Eid al-Adha
Youth Day (SA) (observed)

18 Tuesday

19 Wednesday

Juneteenth

20 Thursday

Summer Solstice

21 Friday

22 Saturday ◯

Windrush Day (UK)

23 Sunday

June

24 Monday

25 Tuesday

26 Wednesday

27 Thursday

28 Friday

Matariki Day (NZ)

29 Saturday

30 Sunday

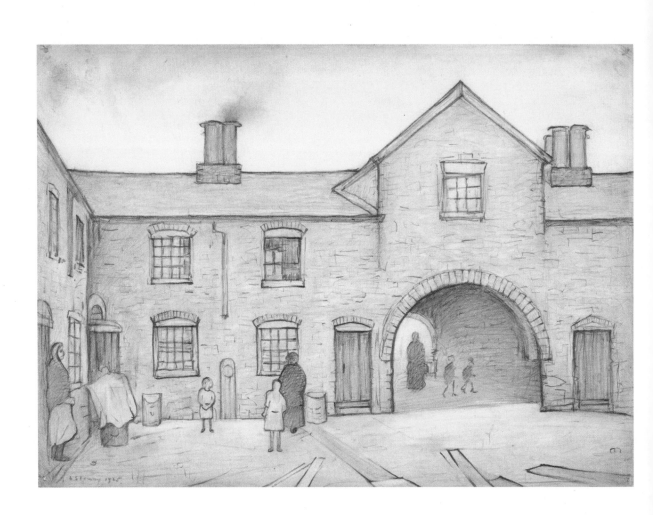

WEEK 27

July

---

1 Monday

Canada Day

2 Tuesday

---

3 Wednesday

---

4 Thursday

Independence Day (USA)

● 5 Friday

---

6 Saturday

---

7 Sunday

Islamic New Year
Muḥarram

Old Houses, Flint, 1925
Pencil on paper

July

8 Monday

9 Tuesday

10 Wednesday

11 Thursday

12 Friday

Battle of the Boyne (N. Ireland)

13 Saturday

◑

Tisha B'Av

14 Sunday

North James Henry Street, Salford, 1956
Pencil on paper

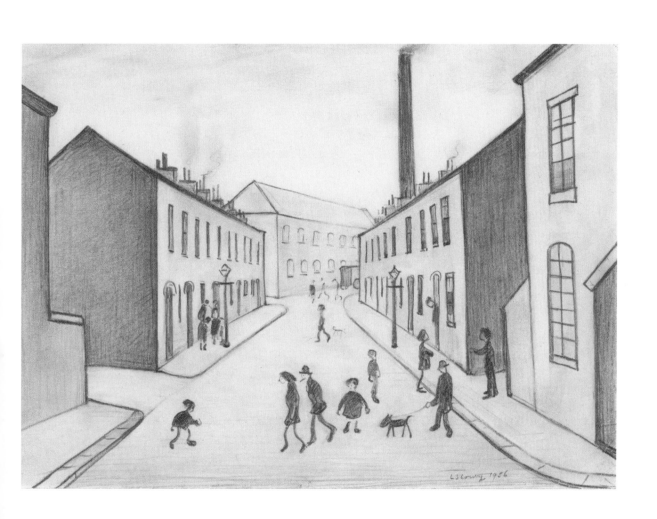

July

15 Monday

Marine Day (Japan)

16 Tuesday

17 Wednesday

18 Thursday

19 Friday

20 Saturday

21 Sunday ○

July

22 Monday

23 Tuesday

24 Wednesday

25 Thursday

26 Friday

27 Saturday

28 Sunday

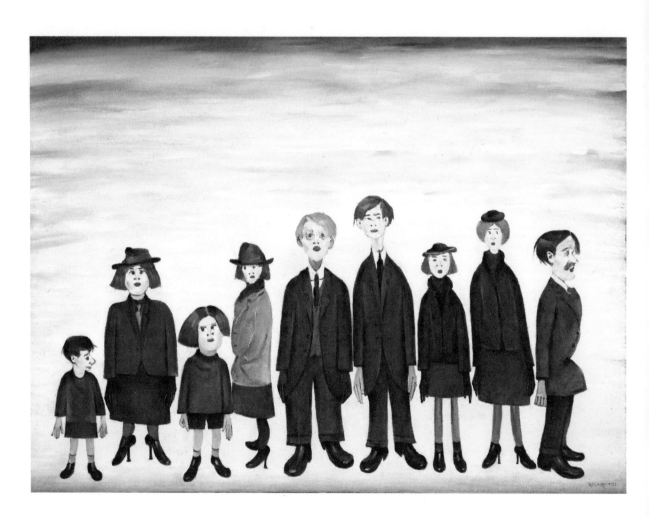

July/August

29 Monday

30 Tuesday

31 Wednesday

1 Thursday

2 Friday

3 Saturday

● 4 Sunday

The Funeral Party, 1953
Oil on canvas

August

5 Monday

August Bank Holiday (Éire)
Summer Bank Holiday (Scot)

6 Tuesday

7 Wednesday

8 Thursday

9 Friday

National Women's Day (SA)

10 Saturday

11 Sunday

Mountain Day (Japan)

By St Philip's Church, Salford, 1926
Pencil on paper

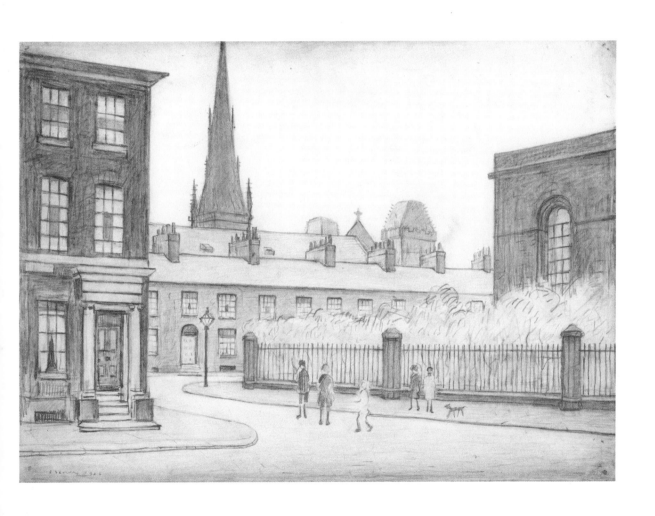

August

12 Monday

◑

Mountain Day (Japan) (observed)

13 Tuesday

14 Wednesday

15 Thursday

16 Friday

17 Saturday

18 Sunday

WEEK **34**

August

○

19 Monday

Raksha Bandhan

20 Tuesday

21 Wednesday

22 Thursday

23 Friday

24 Saturday

25 Sunday

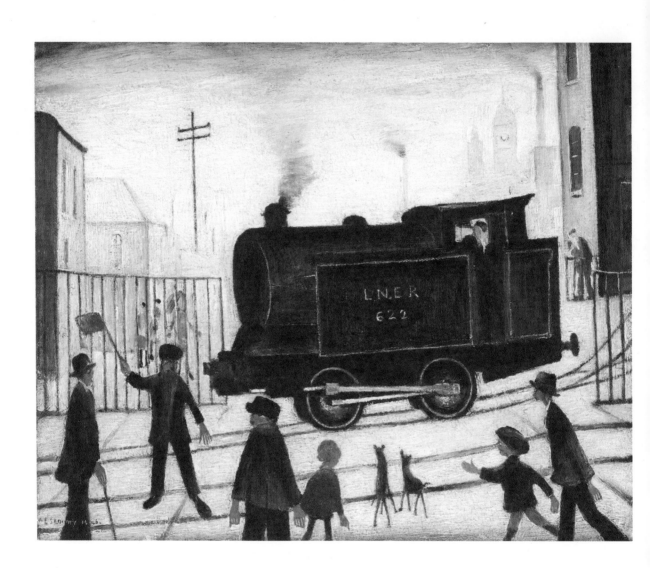

August/September

26 Monday

Krishna Janmashtami
Summer Bank Holiday (UK except Scot)

27 Tuesday

28 Wednesday

29 Thursday

30 Friday

31 Saturday

1 Sunday

Father's Day (AU, NZ)

Level Crossing, 1946
Oil on canvas

September

2 Monday

3 Tuesday ●

4 Wednesday

5 Thursday

6 Friday

7 Saturday

Ganesh Chaturthi

8 Sunday

Grandparents Day (USA, Canada)

An Old Farm, 1943
Oil on board

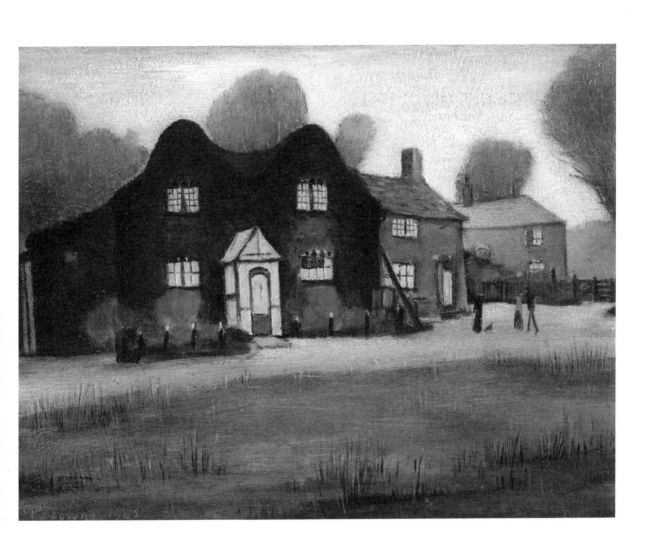

September

9 Monday

10 Tuesday

11 Wednesday

12 Thursday

13 Friday

14 Saturday

15 Sunday

September

---

16 Monday

Respect for the Aged Day (Japan)
Birthday of the Islamic Prophet Muhammad

---

17 Tuesday

○ 18 Wednesday

Pitru-paksha begins

---

19 Thursday

---

20 Friday

---

21 Saturday

International Day of Peace

---

22 Sunday

Autumn Equinox

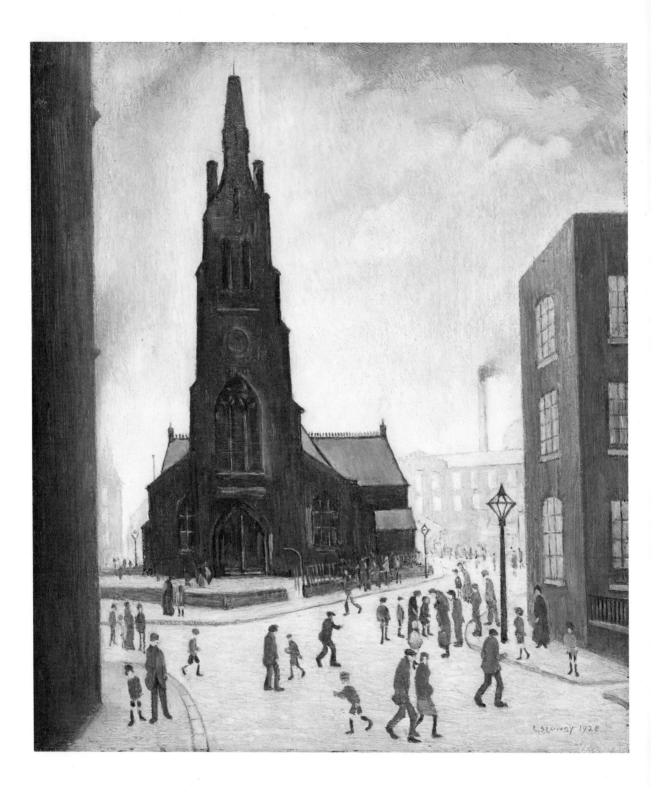

September

23 Monday

24 Tuesday

Heritage Day (SA)

25 Wednesday

26 Thursday

27 Friday

28 Saturday

29 Sunday

A Street Scene (St Simon's Church), 1928
Oil on board

September/October

30 Monday

1 Tuesday

2 Wednesday

●

Pitru-paksha ends

3 Thursday

Sharad Navaratri begins
Jewish New Year (Rosh Hashanah) begins

4 Friday

Jewish New Year (Rosh Hashanah) ends

5 Saturday

6 Sunday

Two People, 1962
Oil on board

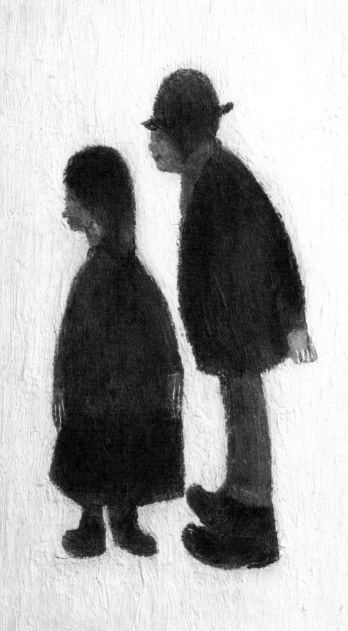

L.S. LOWRY 1963

October

7 Monday

8 Tuesday

9 Wednesday

10 Thursday ◑

11 Friday

12 Saturday

Dussehra
Sharad Navaratri ends
Day of Atonement (Yom Kippur)

13 Sunday

October

---

14 Monday

Sports Day (Japan)
Thanksgiving Day (Canada)
Indigenous Peoples' Day, Columbus Day (USA)

---

15 Tuesday

---

16 Wednesday

○ 17 Thursday

First Day of Sukkot (Feast of Tabernacles)

---

18 Friday

---

19 Saturday

---

20 Sunday

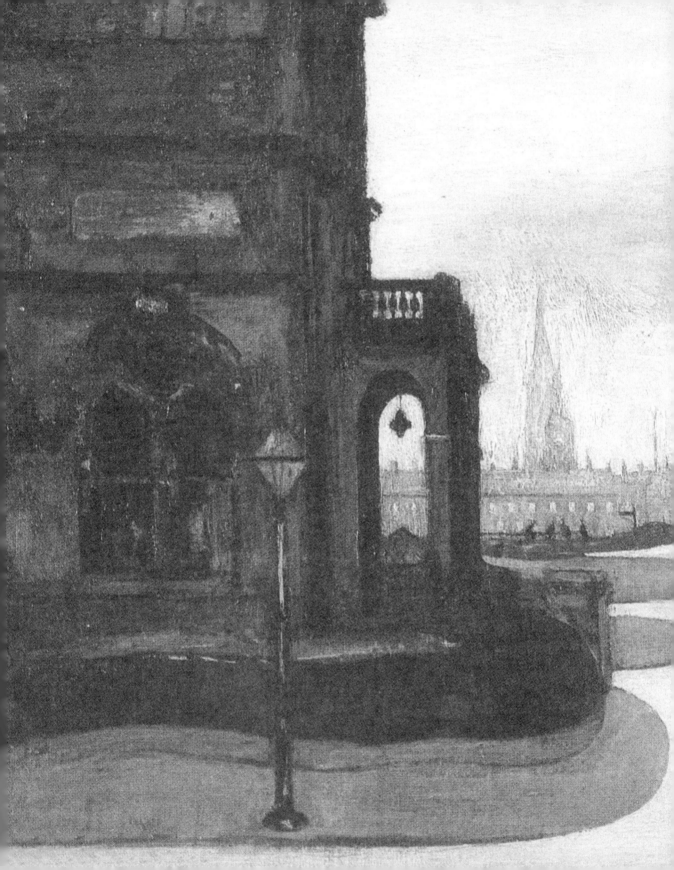

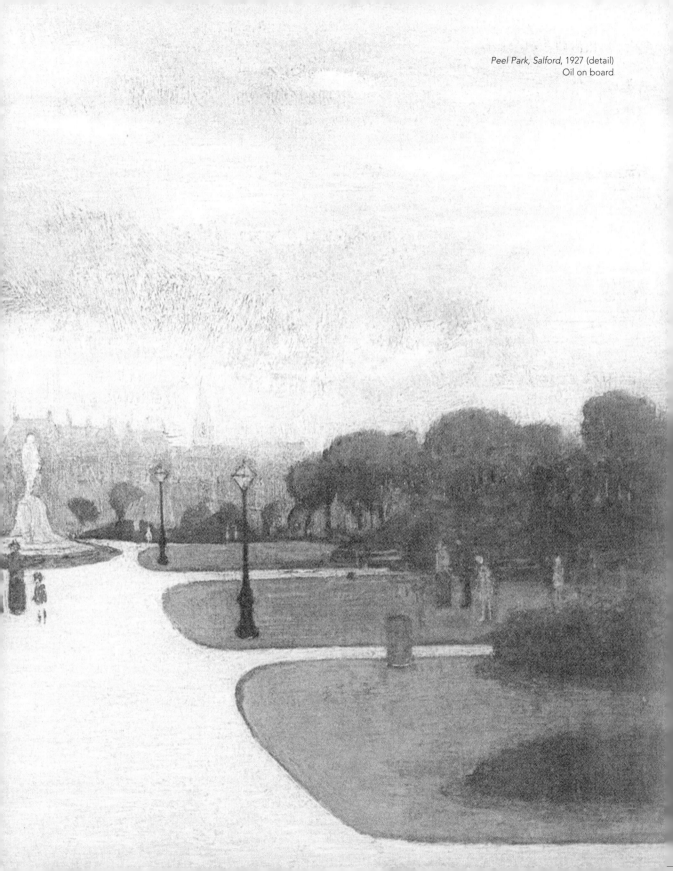

Peel Park, Salford, 1927 (detail)
Oil on board

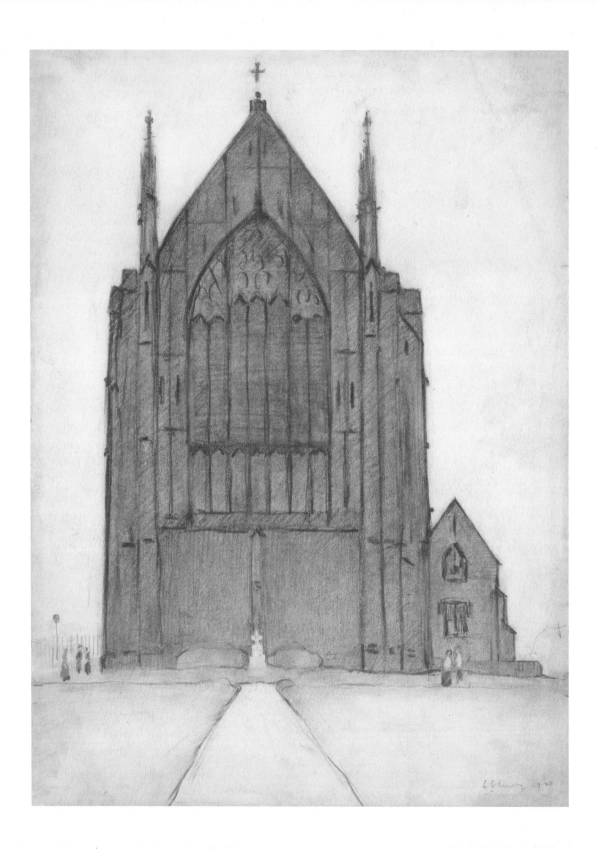

October

21 Monday

22 Tuesday

23 Wednesday

Last Day of Sukkot (Feast of Tabernacles)

24 Thursday

Shemini Atzeret

25 Friday

Simchat Torah

26 Saturday

27 Sunday

British Summer Time ends

St Augustine's Church, Pendlebury, 1930
Pencil on paper

October/November

28 Monday

Labour Day (NZ)
October Bank Holiday (Éire)

29 Tuesday

30 Wednesday

31 Thursday

Halloween

1 Friday

●

Diwali
All Saints' Day
Bandi Chhor Divas

2 Saturday

Vikram Samvat New Year

3 Sunday

Culture Day (Japan)

November

4 Monday

Culture Day (Japan) (observed)

5 Tuesday

6 Wednesday

7 Thursday

8 Friday

9 Saturday

10 Sunday

Remembrance Sunday

November

---

11 Monday

Remembrance Day
(Armistice Day)
Veterans Day (USA)

---

12 Tuesday

---

13 Wednesday

---

14 Thursday

---

15 Friday   ○

Birthday of Guru Nanak

---

16 Saturday

---

17 Sunday

St Stephen's Church, Salford, 1956
Pencil on paper

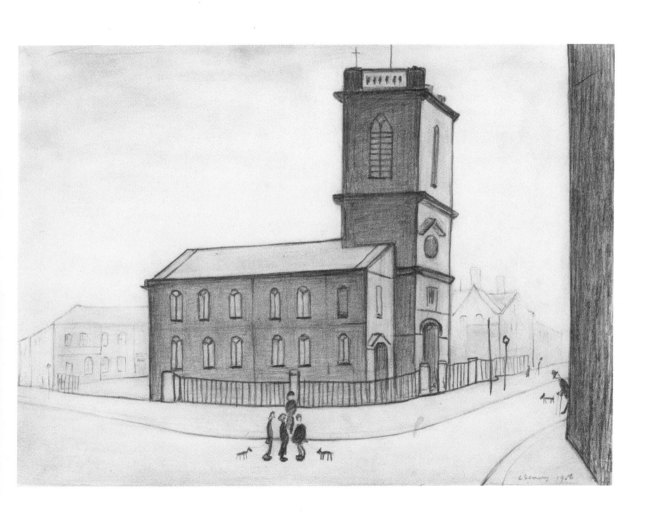

November

18 Monday

19 Tuesday

20 Wednesday

21 Thursday

22 Friday

23 Saturday

Labour Thanksgiving Day (Japan)

24 Sunday

Martyrdom of Guru Tegh Bahadur

November/December

25 Monday

26 Tuesday

27 Wednesday

28 Thursday

Thanksgiving Day (USA)

29 Friday

30 Saturday

St Andrew's Day (Scot)

1 Sunday

Advent Sunday

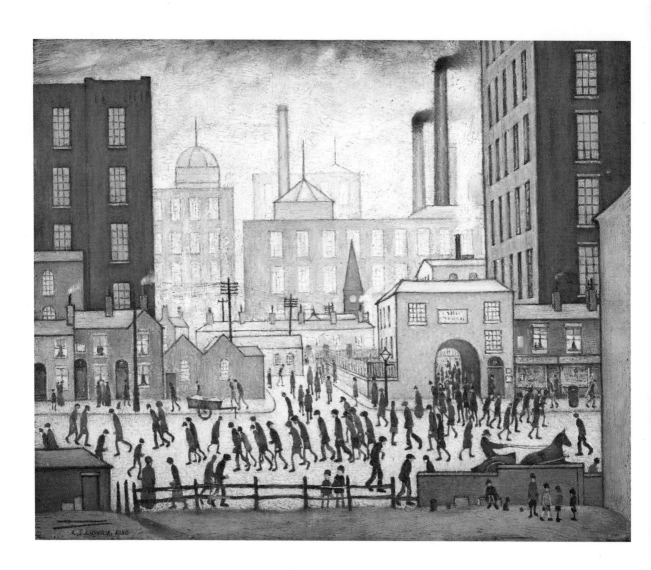

December

2 Monday

St Andrew's Day (Scot) (observed)

3 Tuesday

4 Wednesday

5 Thursday

6 Friday

7 Saturday

◖ 8 Sunday

Bodhi Day

Coming from the Mill, 1930
Oil on canvas

December

9 Monday

10 Tuesday

11 Wednesday

12 Thursday

13 Friday

14 Saturday

15 Sunday

By Christ Church, Salford, 1926
Pencil on paper

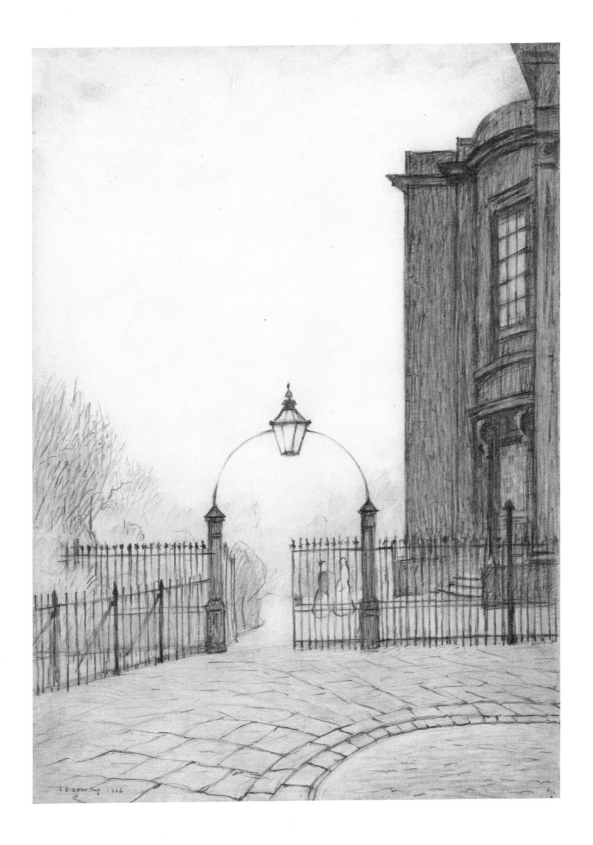

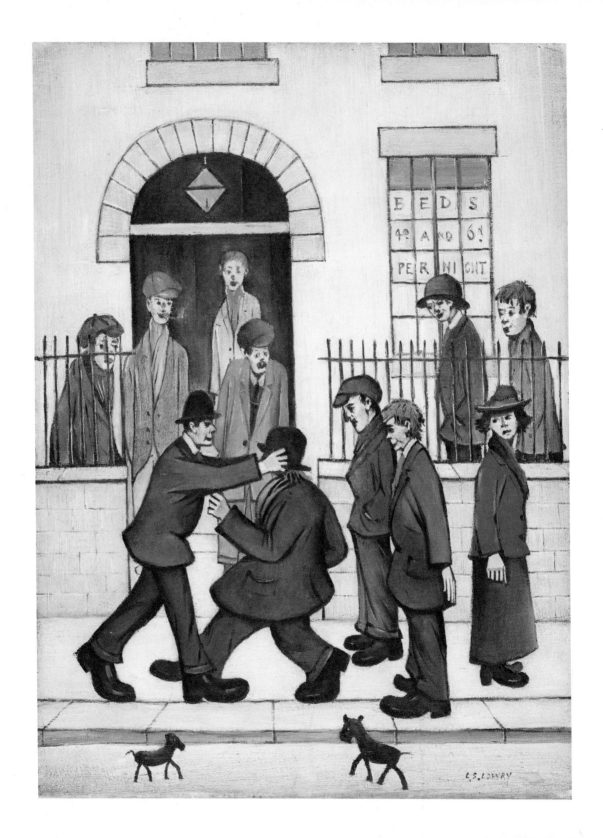

December

16 Monday

Day of Reconciliation (SA)

17 Tuesday

18 Wednesday

19 Thursday

20 Friday

21 Saturday

Winter Solstice

22 Sunday

A Fight, c. 1935
Oil on canvas

December

23 Monday

24 Tuesday

Christmas Eve

25 Wednesday

Christmas Day

26 Thursday

Boxing Day
Hanukkah begins
Day of Goodwill (SA)
St Stephen's Day (Éire)

27 Friday

28 Saturday

29 Sunday

Great Ancoats Street, Manchester, 1930
Pencil on paper

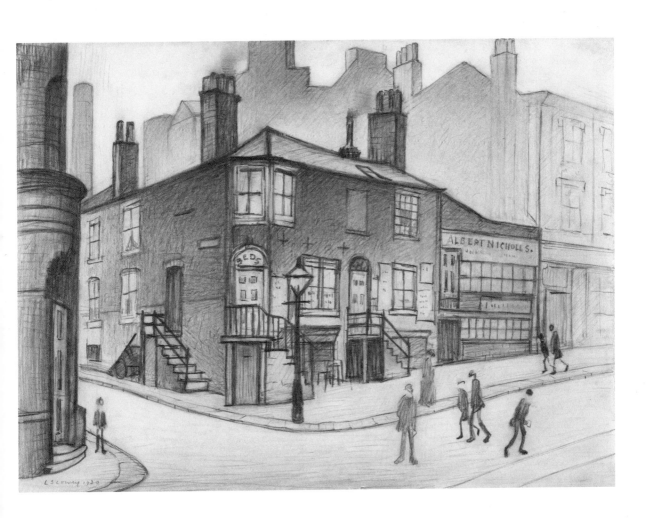

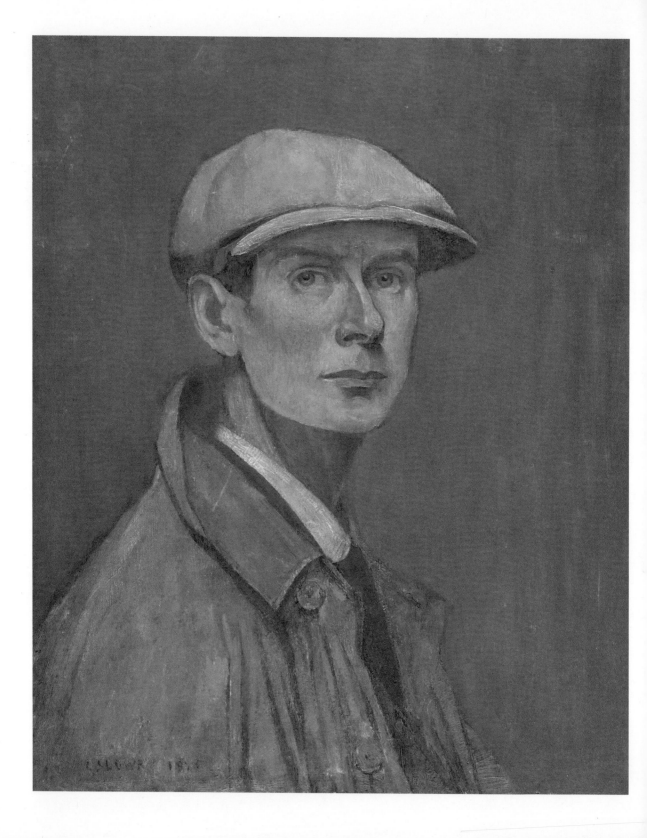

December/January

● 30 Monday

31 Tuesday

New Year's Eve

1 Wednesday

New Year's Day

2 Thursday

Hanukkah ends
Public Holiday (Scot, NZ)

3 Friday

4 Saturday

5 Sunday

Self Portrait, 1925
Oil on board

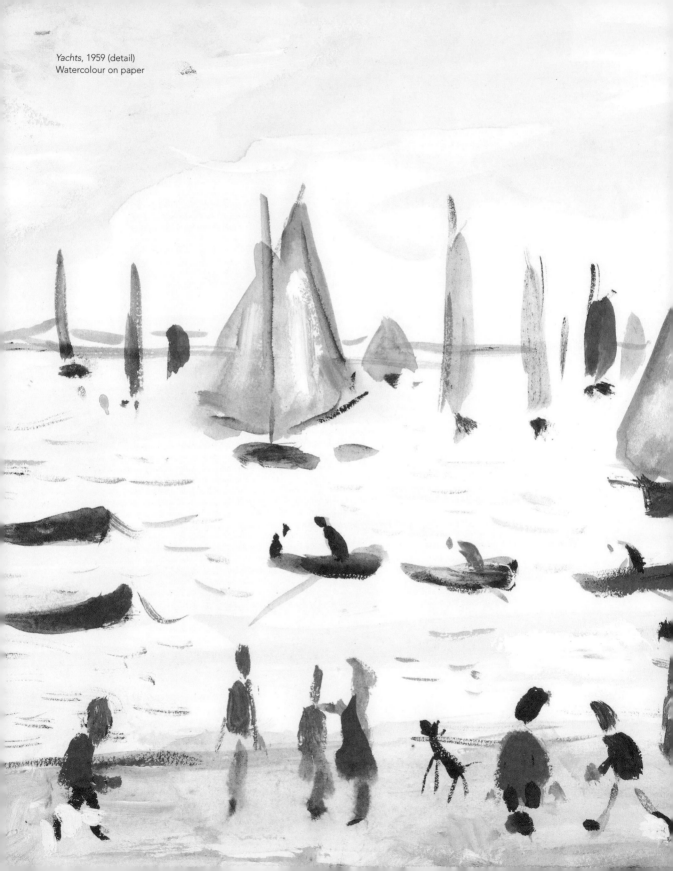

Yachts, 1959 (detail)
Watercolour on paper

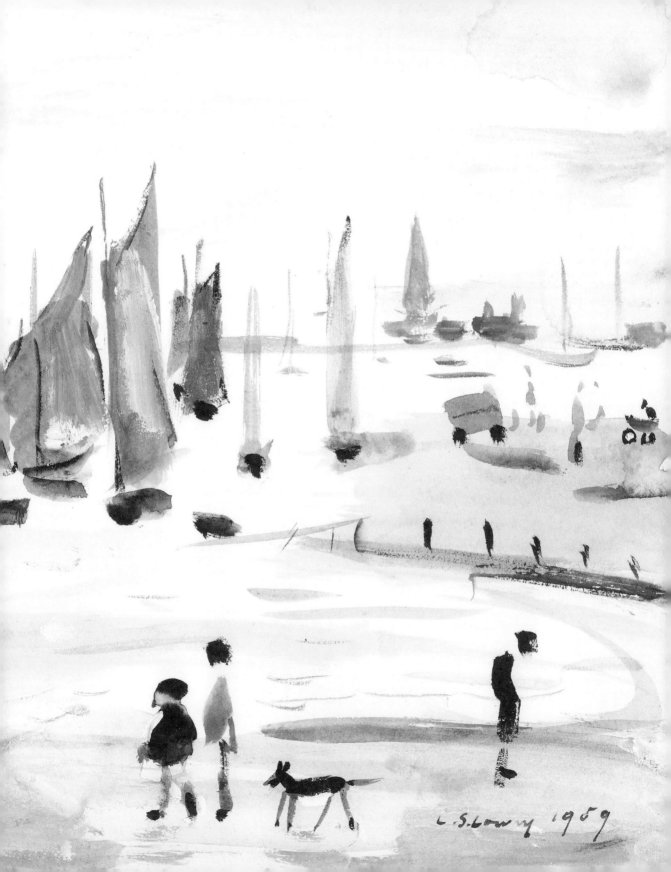

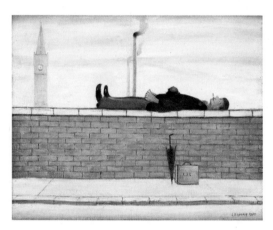

Man Lying on a Wall, 1957
by L.S. Lowry (1887–1976)
© The Lowry Collection, Salford